· WEIRD SCIENCE ·

PLANTS AND FUNGI

HOW THE HECK DOES THAT WORK?!

VIRGINIA LOH-HAGAN

45th Parallel Press

Published in the United States of America by Cherry Lake Publishing Group
Ann Arbor, Michigan
www.cherrylakepublishing.com

Reading Adviser: Beth Walker Gambro, MS, Ed., Reading Consultant, Yorkville, IL
Book Designer: Felicia Macheske

Photo Credits: © Drawlab19/Shutterstock, cover, 1; © Potapov Alexander/Shutterstock, cover, 1; © Andrey
Smirnov/Shutterstock, cover, back cover, 1, 3; © Hayati Kayhan/Shutterstock, cover, 1; © arka38/Shutterstock,
cover, 1; © vilax/Shutterstock, back cover; © Susii/Shutterstock, back cover, 11; © GooseFro/Shutterstock, back
cover; © Roman Mikhailiuk/Shutterstock, 4; © Bodor Tivadar/Shutterstock, 5; © xpixel/Shutterstock, 6; © Take
Photo/Shutterstock, 7; © cembhcvn/Shutterstock, 8; © AlessandroZocc/Shutterstock, 10; © irin-k/Shutterstock, 11;
© Joey Santini/Shutterstock, 12; © RazorGraphix/Shutterstock, 13; © Yurii Andreichyn/Shutterstock, 14; © Georgy
Dzyura/Shutterstock, 15; © BB-Pix/Shutterstock, 16; © Tasha Drik/Shutterstock, 17; © Foxyliam/Shutterstock, 17;
© Sofiaworld/Shutterstock, 18; © Hein Nouwens/Shutterstock, 19; © Buntoon Rodseng/Shutterstock, 19; © Paz
Cometa Photography/Shutterstock, 20; © Robles Designery/Shutterstock, 21; © Drawlab19/Shutterstock, 22;
© Montree Nanta | Dreamstime.com, 23; © Sugrit Jiranarak/Shutterstock, 24; © Fine Art Studio/Shutterstock, 26;
© CkyBe/Shutterstock, 26; © Petar B photography/Shutterstock, 27; © JurateBuiviene/Shutterstock, 28;
© vladsilver/Shutterstock, 30; © trancedrumer/Shutterstock, 31

45th Parallel Press is an imprint of Cherry Lake Publishing Group.

Library of Congress Cataloging-in-Publication Data

Names: Loh-Hagan, Virginia, author.
Title: Weird science : plants and fungi / by Virginia Loh-Hagan.
Description: Ann Arbor, Michigan : Cherry Lake Publishing, 2021.
  | Series: How the heck does that work?!
Identifiers: LCCN 2021004912 (print) | LCCN 2021004913 (ebook)
  | ISBN 9781534187627 (hardcover) | ISBN 9781534189027 (paperback)
  | ISBN 9781534190429 (pdf) | ISBN 9781534191822 (ebook)
Subjects: LCSH: Plant anatomy—Juvenile literature. | Plants—Juvenile
  literature. | Fungi—Anatomy—Juvenile literature.
Classification: LCC QK671 .L64 2021 (print) | LCC QK671 (ebook) | DDC
  571.3/2—dc23
LC record available at https://lccn.loc.gov/2021004912
LC ebook record available at https://lccn.loc.gov/2021004913

Cherry Lake Publishing Group would like to acknowledge the work of the Partnership for 21st Century Learning,
a Network of Battelle for Kids. Please visit *http://www.battelleforkids.org/networks/p21* for more information.

Printed in the United States of America
Corporate Graphics

Dr. Virginia Loh-Hagan is an author, university professor, and former classroom teacher.
She's currently the Director of the Asian Pacific Islander Desi American Resource Center at
San Diego State University. She has fruit orchards and vegetable gardens at her house. She
lives in San Diego with her very tall husband and very naughty dogs.

TABLE OF CONTENTS

At night, plants take in oxygen.
They "breathe" out carbon dioxide.

INTRODUCTION

All kinds of weird science happen in plants. Plants are living things. They keep us alive.

Plants are food. They feed you. Plants also feed the animals you eat.

Plants help you breathe. Plants undergo **photosynthesis**. They use energy from the Sun. They change carbon dioxide into oxygen. You breathe oxygen.

Plants clean the air. Too much carbon dioxide is bad. Plants remove it from the air. Plants can help stop global warming.

Plants are used for many things. People use plants to build houses. People use plants for fuel. People also use plants for medicine.

Botany is the science of plants. Botanists are plant scientists. They study plant life. They study how to make plants grow better. They study how to better use plants.

The world is filled with different kinds of plants. There are trees. There are fruits and vegetables. There are weeds and grasses. There are flowers.

Fungi are special. They're not animals or plants. They don't use photosynthesis. Fungi get their energy from other organisms. They feed off other plants, animals, or decaying material like fallen leaves. They're great recyclers! Fungi include mushrooms and molds. They also include the yeast you use to make bread.

Dare to learn more about plant and fungi science! So much is going on. How the heck does it all work?

Fungi used to be labeled as plants.

The largest animal eaten by a carnivorous plant is a rat.

CHAPTER 1

CARNIVOROUS PLANTS

Do you eat meat? If so, you're a **carnivore**. Carnivore means meat-eater. Some plants are carnivorous, like Venus flytraps and cobra lilies.

Carnivorous plants catch and eat bugs. More than 600 **species** of carnivorous plants exist. Species means groups. Carnivorous plants are all over the world. They live in areas with poor soil. They need a better food source. They eat meat to grow stronger and faster.

Many carnivorous plants have pretty flowers. This is how they attract bugs. The plants then trap the bugs. These plants have different ways of trapping bugs.

Snap traps move very quickly.

Some carnivorous plants have sticky **tentacles**. Tentacles are long arms. Some carnivorous plants have sticky leaves. Bugs get trapped in sticky goo. Goo is made by organs called **glands**.

Other carnivorous plants have hairs that point down. These hairs trap bugs. Bugs can't escape. Some carnivorous plants have pools of water that drown bugs.

Some carnivorous plants have snap traps. Their leaves snap shut. They have tiny hairs. Bugs touch a hair. This sets a trigger. The leaf then snaps shut.

To eat bugs, carnivorous plants release **digestive** juice. The juice breaks down the food.

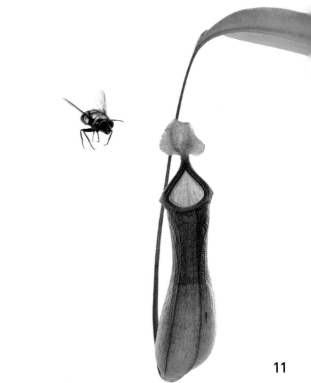

There are other ways plants defend themselves.
They have thorns, spines, and prickles.

CHAPTER 2

POISONOUS PLANTS

Have you ever touched poison ivy? It has a poisonous oil in its leaves, stems, and roots. It's very sticky. It attaches to anything it touches. It causes an itchy skin rash. It causes blisters. It can spread everywhere. This poison protects the plant.

Poisonous plants **evolved** to make poisonous chemicals. Evolve means to change over time. Plants are stuck in the ground. This makes them helpless. They're easily eaten by animals and humans. But some plants evolved by making poisons. This is how they protect themselves. They don't want to be eaten.

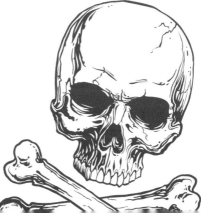

Even WEIRDER PLANT SCIENCE!

- Plants can talk to each other. Some plants use their flowers and leaves to communicate. Flowers and leaves give off chemical signals. These signals attract bugs. They come to get nectar. Flowers and leaves also send signals to warn other plants of dangers. Other plants use their roots to talk. Threads in fungi link plant roots. They share nutrients. Nutrients include proteins and vitamins.

- Honey mushrooms are the world's largest and oldest organisms. They have thick black threads called rhizomorphs. These rhizomorphs spread out. They grow long and thin underground. They eat tree roots. This kills the trees. The largest honey mushroom is in Oregon. It is about 3.4 miles (5.5 kilometers) long. It is thought to be about 8,650 years old!

- Scientists are creating plant cyborgs. Cyborgs are living things with electronic power. Plants create energy from sunlight. Plant cyborgs capture more energy than natural plants. They're used to give energy to robots and machines.

Some plants are **phototoxic**. Their poisons are dangerous in the Sun. The giant hogweed is a flowering plant. It has poisonous sap that looks like clear water. The sap can lead to burns on the skin. In sunlight, this causes lasting burns. Sunlight triggers the poison. It creates energy. The skin takes in that energy. This energy sparks the poison. The poison attacks skin cells.

Some poisonous plants cause sickness or death. They shouldn't be eaten. Death cap mushrooms are deadly. Their poison is a mix of several other poisons. Eating one of these mushrooms could kill a person. Its poisons attack the liver and kidneys.

If giant hogweed sap gets in eyes, it causes blindness.

Ancient Egyptians and Greeks used willow
tree bark to treat various sicknesses.

CHAPTER 3

HEALING PLANTS

Do you take medicine when you're sick? Some plants are used to heal. Medicinal plants are used all over the world. People add them to food. They make teas. They rub them into **wounds**. Wounds are open cuts. These plants solve all types of health problems.

Aloe vera is an example. It's used to cure burns. It has healthy acids. This means it fights **inflammation**. Inflammation causes pain, redness, and swelling. It holds in water. This makes skin soft. Aloe vera triggers the growth of **collagen**. Collagen is a connective tissue. It helps keep the skin firm and flexible. Aloe vera also has vitamins. They keep skin healthy and keep out germs.

Plants make hundreds of chemicals. They make these chemicals for different reasons. These chemicals are active. They interact with living things. They can cause and cure sicknesses. Scientists **extract** these chemicals. Extract means to take out. Scientists grind down plants. They break down the chemicals into compounds. They separate the compounds. They identify each compound. They do tests to learn what each compound can do. They use these compounds to make medicine.

In some cases, scientists use plant poison as medicine. Foxglove is a poisonous plant. It attacks the heart. But scientists turned it into a medicine. They use it to treat heart problems.

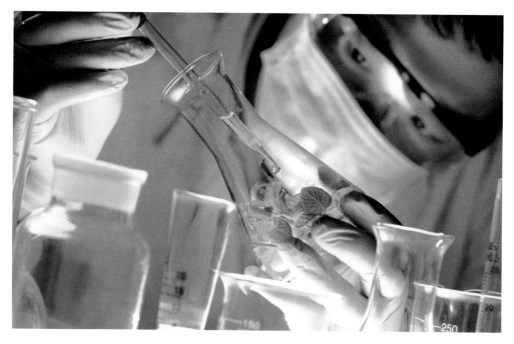

Different plants cure different problems.

UNSOLVED MYSTERY

Rainforests are areas with tall trees. They have warm weather and a lot of rainfall. They're found in Africa, Asia, Australia, and Central and South America. The world's largest rainforest is the Amazon rainforest. It follows the Amazon River through 9 South American countries. The Amazon has many diverse animals and plants. It has more species than any other place. More than 3 million species live there. The Amazon has plants and animals that haven't been discovered yet. The rainforest is close to the equator. This means the forest has warm weather all the time. The equator is an imaginary circle around Earth. It is equally distant from the North and South Poles. There's lots of sun and rain near the equator. The rainforest trees provide safe homes for plants and animals. But there's even more diversity than expected. Species usually compete for resources. This means some species would take over others. But this doesn't seem to happen in the Amazon or most rainforests. Scientists don't know why.

Young plants undergo guttation
more than older plants.

CHAPTER 4

OOZING PLANTS

Did you know plants can bleed? The bleeding tooth fungus oozes. It bleeds bright red drops. These red drops can be used for medicine. They stop bleeding and fight germs.

Oozing is caused by **guttation**. Guttation involves ejecting extra water. It happens at night or early morning. This is when soil is the wettest. Roots take in a lot of water at this time. They may take in too much. Pressure builds up. Leaves and stems have tiny openings. Water drops are pushed out through these openings.

TEST IT OUT!

Plant cells respire. Respire means to breathe. If plants stop respiring, they die. Respiration creates the energy needed to live. Plants take in oxygen and release carbon dioxide. They don't have lungs like animals. They respire through stomata. Stomata are small openings on leaves. Learn more about plant respiration.

Materials

- Large glass bowl
- Warm water
- Large leaf (freshly picked)
- Small rock

1. Fill a large glass bowl with warm water.

2. Go outside. Pull a large leaf from a tree or plant. Make sure the leaf is alive.

3. Put the leaf in the bowl. Put the small rock on top of it. Make sure it's fully underwater.

4. Put the bowl in a sunny spot. Plants use sunlight. They convert it to energy.

5. Wait a few hours.

6. Watch the leaf. Small bubbles will form. It's much like how people make bubbles when breathing underwater. The bubbles are air. This shows plant respiration.

Guttation lets plants restore balance. It controls how much water plants take in. Without guttation, plants would break or even explode. Guttation also keeps roots from rotting. It drains the soil around them.

Tropical areas are warm and rainy. In these areas, guttation is common. The air is thick with water. If you're in the jungle, you may feel rain. But it's not rain. Those drops are from guttation.

Many common plants go through guttation. Grasses push out water. Some food crops do as well. These include tomatoes and strawberries.

Guttation looks like plant sweat.

Dinoflagellates give off light to attract bigger predators. Big predators eat the smaller predators that may eat the plankton.

CHAPTER 5

GLOWING PLANTS

Have you ever seen anything glow in the dark? Some plants glow. They have **bioluminescence**. Bioluminescence is the ability to make and give off light.

Plankton are tiny plants and animals. They live in water. They float in tides and waves. Dinoflagellates are a type of plankton. In Puerto Rico, there are millions of dinoflagellates. When disturbed, they give off a blue glow.

More than 70 species of glowing mushrooms live on Earth. Foxfire plants live in rotting wood. They have a blue-green glow. They glow for several reasons. One reason is to scare off **predators**. Predators are hunters.

SCIENTIST SPOTLIGHT

Pauline Estrada is a young scientist. She's from Fresno, California. Fresno is in central California. It's farm country. It faces dry periods called droughts. It's hard to grow crops during droughts. Pauline wanted to help farmers. At age 12, she created a robot. The robot has a camera system. It takes pictures of plants using infrared rays. Infrared rays are a special type of light. It is invisible to the human eye. The robot's camera system shows if plants are getting enough water. It checks plant temperatures and dryness levels. Pauline's tool is useful to farmers. It lets them know when to water their crops. That helps them save water. Pauline said, "Seeing the impact that drought had on our agriculture here in Fresno really inspired me to create a project in order to help these farmers measure water use more efficiently and maximize their yield and detect drought stress."

Most species glow only at night. But some do it all the time to release extra energy.

Glowing organisms have light energy. They use 2 compounds to produce it. These are luciferin and luciferase. Luciferin mixes with oxygen. Luciferase then sparks a chemical reaction. The reaction produces light.

Glowing plants are rare. Some may have the cells to glow. But they don't have cells to spark a reaction. Scientists found a way to make plants glow. They took glowing cells and added them to plants. The plants glowed dimly. Scientists are working on this process.

Glowing plants could save electricity.

Decomposing is faster in warm places.
The process slows down in cold places.

CHAPTER 6

ROTTING PLANTS

Did you know that plants die? Nature recycles. Plants are part of the circle of life.

When plants die, they **decompose**. Decompose means to break down. Plants rot. They're broken into tiny pieces. Those pieces become nutrients. Living things need nutrients. Dead plants become part of the soil. The soil feeds living plants. Living plants get nutrients from the soil. In this way, living plants eat dead plants.

Fungi and bacteria are decomposers. When plants die, the decomposers get to work. They help break down dead plants. using chemical reactions. They release nutrients. More decomposers join in. They do this to live and grow.

Without carbon dioxide, Earth's oceans would be frozen solid. This and other gases help trap a portion of the Sun's heat.

Carbon is a chemical element found in every living thing. It's part of the carbon cycle. The cycle starts with plants. Plants undergo photosynthesis to make their own foods. They create plant sugars. These sugars help them grow. They give them energy. Animals eat these plants. They digest the sugar molecules. When animals breathe and poop, this carbon is released back into the soil for plants. When plants die, carbon and other elements stay in their **fibers**. Fibers are plant threads. Decomposers break down the fibers. They release carbon into the air, soil, and water. Living things then use the carbon.

Too much carbon in the atmosphere causes global warming. Global warming is harmful to many animals and plants. Understanding the carbon cycle helps us save the planet.

GLOSSARY

bioluminescence (bye-oh-loo-meh-NEH-suhnts) the ability to make and give off light

botany (BOT-uh-nee) the study of the science of plants

carnivore (KAR-nuh-vor) an animal or plant that eats meat

collagen (KAH-luh-juhn) a connective tissue

decompose (dee-kuhm-POZE) to rot or decay

digestive (dye-JEH-stiv) having to do with breaking down food

evolved (ee-VOLVD) changed over time

extract (ek-STRAKT) to pull out

fibers (FYE-burs) long, thin strands of material made by plants

fungi (FUHN-jye) a group of living organisms that make up their own kingdom of living things

glands (GLANDZ) body organs that secrete substances

guttation (guh-TAY-shuhn) secretion of water drops from leaves

inflammation (in-fluh-MAY-shuhn) a bodily response to injury that causes pain, heat, redness, and swelling

photosynthesis (foh-toh-SIN-thuh-siss) the process by which green plants use sunlight to turn carbon dioxide and water into food

phototoxic (foh-toh-TAK-sik) poisoned by sunlight

plankton (PLANGK-tuhn) tiny organisms that float in the ocean

predators (PRED-uh-turs) animals or plants that hunt other animals for food

species (spee-SHEEZ) groups of animals or plants that share the same traits

tentacles (TEN-tuh-kuhls) long, flexible arms

wounds (WOONDZ) open cuts

LEARN MORE

Jose, Sarah. *Trees, Leaves, Flowers, and Seeds: A Visual Encyclopedia of the Plant Kingdom*. New York, NY: DK Publishing, 2019.

Stone, Brandy. *Gardening for Kids: Learn, Grow, and Get Messy with Fun STEAM Projects*. Emeryville, CA: Rockridge Press, 2020.

INDEX